HEALTHY VEGAN DESSERTS RECIPES

More than 50 Exciting Quick and Easy New Vegan Recipes for Cookies and Pies, Cupcakes and Cakes--and More!

Daniel Smith

Table of Contents

HEALTHY VEGAN DESSERTS RECIPES 1

MORE THAN 50 EXCITING QUICK AND EASY NEW VEGAN RECIPES FOR COOKIES AND PIES, CUPCAKES AND CAKES-- AND MORE! 1

DANIEL SMITH 1

TABLE OF CONTENTS 3

INTRODUCTION 8
- Coconut Cake with Chocolate Ganache 10
- Orange Cranberry Cake 13
- Marbled Banana Bread 16
- Chocolate Mint Cake 19
- Red Wine Chocolate Cake 22
- Coconut and Orange Cake 25
- Applesauce Spice Cake 28
- Red Velvet Beet Cake 31
- Simple Chocolate Cake 34
- Coconut Bread 36
- Ginger and Applesauce Cake 39
- Walnut Carrot Cake 42
- Strawberry Cake 45
- Banana Blueberry Cake 48
- Cinnamon Swirl Cake 51
- Banana Coffee Cake 54
- Date and Walnut Cake 56
- Chocolate Zucchini Cake 59
- Cranberry Carrot Cake 61
- Orange Poppy Seed Cake 64
- Lemon Poppy Seed Cake 67
- Chocolate Banana Carrot Cake 69
- Coconut Cake with Caramel Sauce 71
- Cardamom Carrot Cake 73
- Mandarin Cake 76
- Chocolate Orange Cake 79
- Peach Upside-Down Cake 81
- Pineapple Upside-Down Cake 84
- Raspberry Chocolate Cake 86
- Cherry, Walnut and Banana Cake 88
- Cherry Snack Cake 90

Chocolate Zucchini Mud Cake 92
Vegan Basic Vanilla Cake.. 94
Olive Oil Rosemary Semolina Cake 97
Apfelkuchen 99
Blueberry Chocolate Cake 102
Blueberry Whole Wheat Muffins 104
Chocolate Chip Cookie Dough Muffins.. 107
Banana and Sunflower Muffins 109
Fudgy Chocolate Muffins 111
Tropical Coconut Muffins... 114
Melon Muffins 117
Multigrain Muffins.. 119
Almond Cranberry Muffins 121
Ginger and Banana Muffins... 124
Plum Muffins... 126
Blackberry Corn Muffins 128
Sweet Potato Ginger Muffins... 130
Quinoa Raspberry Muffins... 133
Applesauce Cardamom Muffins... 135

© Copyright 2021 by Daniel Smith - All rights reserved.

The following Book is reproduced below with the goal of providing information that is as accurate and reliable as possible. Regardless, purchasing this Book can be seen as consent to the fact that both the publisher and the author of this book are in no way experts on the topics discussed within and that any recommendations or suggestions that are made herein are for entertainment purposes only. Professionals should be consulted as needed prior to undertaking any of the action endorsed herein.

This declaration is deemed fair and valid by both the American Bar Association and the Committee of Publishers Association and is legally binding throughout the United States.

Furthermore, the transmission, duplication, or reproduction of any of the following work including specific information will be considered an illegal act irrespective of if it is done electronically or in print. This extends to creating a secondary or tertiary copy of the work or a recorded copy and is only allowed with the express written consent from the Publisher. All additional right reserved.

The information in the following pages is broadly considered a truthful and accurate account of facts and as such, any inattention, use, or misuse of the information in question by the reader will render any resulting actions solely under their purview. There are no scenarios in which the publisher or the original author of this work can be in any fashion deemed liable for any hardship or damages that may befall them after undertaking information described herein.

Additionally, the information in the following pages is intended only for informational purposes and should thus be thought of as universal. As befitting its nature, it is presented without assurance regarding its prolonged validity or interim quality. Trademarks that are mentioned are done without written consent and can in no way be considered an endorsement from the trademark holder.

Introduction

Congratulations on your smart and brilliant move in stepping forward to the prospect of a wonderful and harmonious life with nature! Not everyone chooses to make the biggest and most important change and, for that, I applaud you! Now you are going to be exposed to the world of delicious and creative recipes—101 wonderful vegan desserts. Unlike many prejudices that suggest that vegans don't have desserts at all, this book is going to surprise you!! You will learn that there are dozens of wonderful and nutritious ways to end a meal in a harmonious and healthy way.

Coconut Cake with Chocolate Ganache

This moist and fragrant cake is covered with a silky ganache which gives it an exquisite feel that makes it even more delicious.

Servings: 4-6 dishes

Ingredients:

Cake:

3/4 cup almond butter, room temperature

1 cup sugar

4 tablespoons flax seeds, ground

8 tablespoons water

3/4 cup coconut flour

1 1/2 cup all purpose flour

2/3 cup cocoa powder

1 teaspoon baking powder

1/2 teaspoon baking soda

1 1/4 cup coconut milk

1 teaspoon vanilla extract

1 pinch of salt

Dark chocolate ganache:

5 oz dark chocolate

4 oz coconut cream

1 tablespoon almond butter

Directions:

1. Mix the ground flax seeds with water and let them soak 5-10 minutes.

2. In a bowl, mix the butter and sugar for 4-5 minutes until fluffy and light in color. Stir in the flax seeds and vanilla extract.

3. In another bowl, sift together the flours, cocoa powder with 1 pinch of salt, baking powder and baking soda.

4. Start incorporating the flour into the butter mixture, alternating it with milk. Begin and end with flour. Once all the ingredients are incorporated, turn your mixer to high heat and mix for 2 minutes.

5. Pour the mixture in a greased pan and bake in a preheated oven at 350F for 30-40 minutes.

6. To make the ganache: heat the coconut cream then stir in the chopped chocolate. Mix well to combine then add the butter. Pour the ganache over the cake.

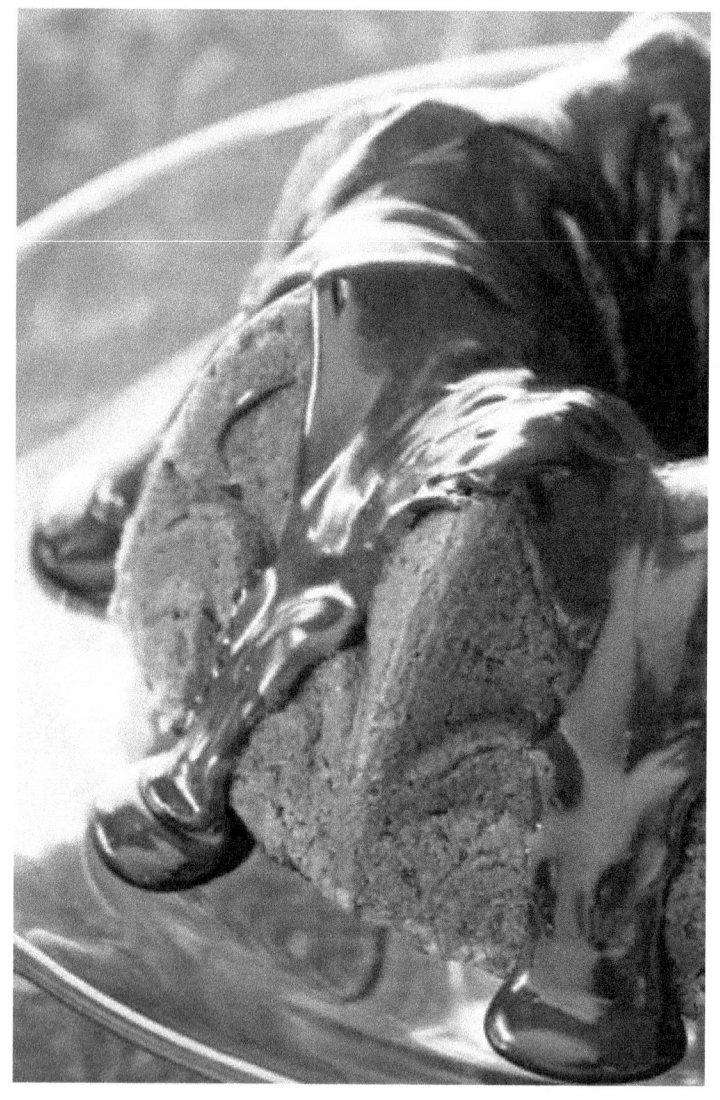

Orange Cranberry Cake

Easy to make and with just a few ingredients, this cake is perfect even for breakfast next to a cup of tea or a glass of warm milk. Simply enjoy its amazing flavors.

Servings: 4-6 dishes

Ingredients:

1 1/2 cup all purpose flour

1 teaspoon baking powder

1 tablespoon orange zest

1 cup sugar

1 cup coconut milk

1/2 cup fresh cranberries

1 pinch of salt

Directions:

1. In a bowl, mix the sugar with the salt, milk and orange zest.

2. Stir in the flour and baking powder then fold in the cranberries.

3. Pour this batter into a small cake pan greased with oil.

4. Bake in a preheated oven at 350F for 30 minutes or until golden brown or fragrant.

Marbled Banana Bread

Banana bread is a classic dessert, often eaten even for breakfast. It is also a very versatile recipe as you can add coconut or chocolate chips and you have a whole new recipe to make and enjoy.

Servings: 4-6 dishes

Ingredients:

1 cup mashed bananas
1/2 cup brown sugar
1 teaspoon vanilla extract
3 tablespoons vegetable oil
1/3 cup soy milk
1 1/4 cup whole wheat flour
1 teaspoon baking soda
1/2 teaspoon baking powder
4 tablespoons cocoa powder
6 tablespoons hot water
1 pinch of salt

Directions:

1. Line a loaf pan with parchment paper and set aside.

2. In a bowl, mix together the bananas, sugar, vanilla, oil and soy milk.

3. In another bowl, combine the whole wheat flour, baking soda and powder, as well as a pinch of salt.

4. Combine the wet ingredients with the dry ingredients and mix until well combined.

5. Divide the batter into two equal parts. In one part, mix 3 tablespoons of water and, in theother, besides the 3 tablespoons of water, add the cocoa powder as well.

6. Pour the batters into your prepared pan, one at a time, then marble the mixture with a skewer.

7. Bake in a preheated oven at 350F for 30-40 minutes.

8. Serve cold with a sprinkle of powdered sugar.

Chocolate Mint Cake

Chocolate cake is a classic, but add a little twist with a bit of mint and you will have a real delight to enjoy.

Servings: 4-6 dishes

Ingredients:

1/4 cup olive oil

1/4 cup melted chocolate

1/4 cup sugar

1 tablespoon flax seeds, ground

2 tablespoons water

1/2 cup flour

1 teaspoon mint extract

1/2 teaspoon baking powder

1 pinch of salt

Directions:

1. In a bowl, mix the flax seeds with water and set aside to soak for 10 minutes.

2. Stir in the sugar, then incorporate the oil and melted chocolate, followed by the flour and baking powder and mint extract, as well as a pinch of salt.

3. Grease a small cake pan with oil and pour in the chocolate batter.

4. Cook in a preheated oven at 350F for 30-40 minutes.

Red Wine Chocolate Cake

Red wine and chocolate is a great combination and this cake is moist and flavorful, delicious for a grown-ups' party or dinner.

Servings: 4-6 dishes

Ingredients:

3 tablespoons flax seeds, ground

6 tablespoons water

1/2 cup brown sugar

6 tablespoons olive oil

3/4 cup red wine

1 teaspoon vanilla extract

1 cup all purpose flour

2 tablespoons cocoa powder

1/2 teaspoon cinnamon

1 teaspoon baking powder

1 pinch of salt

Directions:

1. In a bowl, mix the ground flax seeds with water and let it soak for 5 minutes.

2. Stir in the oil and sugar and mix well until combined.

3. In another bowl, sift together the flour, baking powder, cinnamon, cocoa and salt. Incorporate the dry ingredients into the oil mixture, alternating it with red wine.

4. Grease a 9-inch round pan and pour in the batter.

5. Bake in the preheated oven at 350F for 30-40 minutes. Let cool in the pan then transfer toa serving plate and sprinkle with powdered sugar.

Coconut and Orange Cake

Having a tropical aroma, this cake will exceed your expectations with its moisture and fragrance. If you like coconut, don't hesitate to make it. You will love it.

Servings: 4-6 dishes

Ingredients:

1/2 cup coconut flour

4 tablespoons flax seeds, ground

8 tablespoons water

1/4 cup coconut milk

1/4 cup coconut oil

1/2 cup brown sugar

1 teaspoon orange zest

1 pinch of salt

1 teaspoon baking powder

1/2 teaspoon baking soda

4 tablespoons orange juice

1 pinch of salt

Directions:

1. In a bowl, mix together the flax seeds with water and set aside for 5 minutes.

2. Stir in the sugar, vanilla, orange zest and juice. Add the coconut oil, melted and chilled, then incorporate the coconut flour, baking powder and baking soda, as well as a pinch of salt.

3. Pour the batter into a greased 9-inch cake pan and bake in a preheated oven at 350F for 30-40 minutes

4. Let cool in the pan then sprinkle with powdered sugar and serve cut into slices

Applesauce Spice Cake

Applesauce is very healthy and makes this cake very moist, loaded with autumn flavors, such as walnuts and cinnamon. It will flood your house with lovely flavors while baking.

Servings: 4-6 dishes

Ingredients:

2 cups all purpose flour
3/4 cup sugar
1 teaspoon baking soda
1/2 teaspoon baking powder
1 teaspoon cinnamon
1 teaspoon ground ginger
1/2 cup golden raisins
1/2 cup chopped walnuts
4 tablespoons olive oil
1 1/2 cups applesauce
1 pinch of salt
1 teaspoon vanilla extract

Directions:

1. In a bowl, mix the flour, sugar, baking soda and baking powder, as well as cinnamon and ground ginger.

2. Mix in the raisins and walnuts then stir in the applesauce, olive oil and vanilla extract, as well as a pinch of salt.

3. Pour this batter into a round cake pan lined with baking paper.

4. Bake in a preheated oven at 350F for 30-40 minutes.

5. Let cool in the pan then sprinkle with powdered sugar and serve cut into slices.

Red Velvet Beet Cake

The classic red velvet cake can be made with beets instead of food coloring and you obtain a healthy version of the amazing red velvet cake. It is very suited to kids or people who have to avoid food coloring due to health problems.

Servings: 4-6 dishes

Ingredients:

1 medium size beet, steamed, peeled and pureed

1/3 cup coconut oil

1 cup sugar

1 cup all purpose flour

1/4 cup whole wheat flour

2 tablespoons cocoa powder

1 teaspoon baking powder

1/2 teaspoon baking soda

1 1/4 cup coconut milk

1 teaspoon vanilla extract

1 pinch of salt

Directions:

1. In a bowl, mix well the beet puree with coconut oil then stir in the sugar and vanilla. Sift together the flours, cocoa powder, salt and baking powder and soda.

2. Incorporate this mixture into the beet one, alternating with coconut milk. Start and end with the dry ingredients.

3. Pour the batter into a round cake pan, lined with baking paper.

4. Bake the cake in a preheated oven at 350F for 30 to 40 minutes.

5. Let cool in the pan then transfer to a serving plate and serve powdered with sugar.

Simple Chocolate Cake

Sometimes you want to make something sweet, but you don't want something too difficult to make. And that is when this cake steps in because it's very easy to make and tastes amazing.

Servings: 4-6 dishes

Ingredients:
1 cup all purpose flour
1 cup sugar
4 tablespoons cocoa
1 teaspoon vinegar
1 cup cold water
1 teaspoon vanilla extract
1 pinch of salt
1 teaspoon baking powder

Directions:

1. Simply mix all the ingredients together in a large bowl then pour the batter into a round cake pan, lined with baking paper.

2. Bake in a preheated oven at 350F for 20-30 minutes or until a skewer inserted in the center of the cake comes out clean.

3. Serve sprinkled with powdered sugar.

Coconut Bread

If you are a coconut fan, this bread will be a delight with its strong coconut flavor and amazing texture. Being vegan, it is also healthier than other versions of the same bread.

Servings: 4-6 dishes

Ingredients:

1/2 cup unsweetened applesauce
1 1/3 cup almond or soy milk
1 teaspoon vanilla extract
1 1/3 cups all purpose flour
1 teaspoon baking powder
1/2 teaspoon baking soda
1 teaspoon cinnamon
1 cup sugar
1 1/2 cup sweetened coconut flakes
6 tablespoons coconut oil
1 teaspoon lemon juice
1 pinch of salt

Directions:

1. In a small bowl, mix well the applesauce, milk and vanilla extract.

2. In another bowl, mix together the flour, baking powder and soda, cinnamon and a pinch of salt. Stir in the coconut flakes and sugar then pour in the milk mixture. Give it a good mix to combine well then pour the batter into a round cake pan, lined with baking paper.

3. Bake in a preheated oven at 350F for 30-40 minutes, or until slightly golden brown on the edges and fragrant.

Ginger and Applesauce Cake

Ginger has a strong flavor so make sure you only use a bit in this recipe. Other than that, the cake is delicious and it preserves a lot of moisture from the applesauce.

Servings: 2-4 dishes

Ingredients:

2 cups whole wheat flour

1 cup sugar

2 oz candied ginger, chopped

2 tablespoons cornstarch

1 teaspoon baking soda

1 teaspoon baking powder

1 teaspoon cinnamon

2 1/2 cups applesauce

1 tablespoon lemon juice

1 teaspoon vanilla extract

1 pinch of salt

2 tablespoons maple syrup

Directions:

1. In a bowl, mix together the applesauce, lemon juice and vanilla.

2. Stir in the sugar, flour, cornstarch, baking soda and powder, cinnamon and a pinch of salt. Mix well then fold in the candied ginger.

3. Pour this batter into a round cake pan, lined with parchment paper.

4. Bake the cake in a preheated oven at 350F for 30-40 minutes. To check if it's done, insert a skewer into the center. If it comes out clean, the cake is done, if not, bake it 10 more minutes.

5. Let it cool in the pan then powder it with sugar and serve cut into slices.

Walnut Carrot Cake

Carrot cake with walnuts tastes great because walnuts add a bit of texture, but also an earthy flavor that pairs wonderfully with carrots.

Servings: 4-6 dishes

Ingredients:
10 dates, pits removed
2 cups grated carrots
1/2 cup sweetened applesauce
1/2 cup golden raisins
1 teaspoon cinnamon
1 teaspoon ground ginger
1/2 teaspoon ground cloves
3/4 cup whole wheat flour
1/4 cup all purpose flour
1 teaspoon baking powder
1/2 teaspoon baking soda
1/2 cup walnuts, chopped
1 pinch of salt

Directions:

1. Put the dates in a small blender or food processor and pulse a few times until a paste forms. Transfer them into a bowl then stir in the carrots, applesauce, raisins, cinnamon, ginger and a pinch of salt.

2. Mix until well combined then fold in the flour, baking powder and soda. Spoon the batterinto a greased round cake pan then sprinkle the chopped walnuts on top.

3. Bake in a preheated oven at 350F for 30-40 minutes.

4. Let it cool in the pan and serve sprinkled with powdered sugar.

Strawberry Cake

Strawberries must be one of the most loved fruits worldwide, but they also make excellent desserts, such as this flavorful and crumbly cake.

Servings: 4-6 dishes

Ingredients:

1 1/2 cups all purpose flour

2/3 cup sugar

1/3 cup soy yogurt

1 teaspoon baking soda

2/3 teaspoon baking powder

1 teaspoon vanilla extract

1 cup soy milk

2 cups fresh strawberries, coarsely chopped

2 tablespoons cornstarch

1 pinch of salt

Directions:

1. In a bowl, mix together the flour, sugar, baking powder and soda as well as a pinch of salt. Stir in the yogurt, vanilla and soy milk. Give it a good mix then pour the batter into a round 9 inch cake pan.

2. Mix the strawberries with the cornstarch and sprinkle them on top of the batter.

3. Bake the cake in a preheated oven at 350F for 40-50 minutes.

4. When done, let it cool in the pan then transfer to a serving plate and sprinkle with powdered sugar.

Banana Blueberry Cake

Banana cakes are generally very moist and fragrant, but this cake is even better with the addition of blueberries. Baked to perfection, this cake is a great choice for any party or even a fancy dinner.

Servings: 4-6 dishes

Ingredients:
3 ripe bananas, mashed
1 teaspoon lemon juice
1/2 cup soy milk
1 teaspoon vanilla extract
1/3 cup agave nectar
1/4 cup sugar
2 cups whole wheat flour
1/2 teaspoon baking soda
1/2 teaspoon baking powder
1 cup fresh blueberries
1 pinch of salt

Directions:

1. Grease a 9 inch round cake pan and set aside.

2. In a bowl, mix the soy milk with the lemon juice and let it sit for 5 minutes.

3. Stir in the bananas and agave nectar and sugar and mix well.

4. In another bowl, mix the flour with the baking powder, salt and baking soda. Pour in the banana mixture and give it a good mix. Fold in the blueberries and pour the batter into the prepared pan.

5. Bake the cake in a preheated oven at 350F for 40-50 minutes. Let it cool in the pan then transfer to a serving plate and sprinkle with powdered sugar.

Cinnamon Swirl Cake

Cinnamon can be very strong, but this cake only uses a bit for flavor and creates an amazing swirl that enhances the visual effect of the slice.

Servings: 4-6 dishes

Ingredients:
1 cup all purpose flour
1 cup whole wheat flour
1 teaspoon baking powder
1 teaspoon baking soda
1 teaspoon cinnamon
1/2 teaspoon ground ginger
2 tablespoons flax seeds, ground
4 tablespoons water
1/2 cup soy yogurt
3/4 cup orange juice
1/2 cup soy milk
1/2 cup agave syrup
1/4 cup sugar
1 pinch of salt

Directions:

1. In a small bowl, mix the ground flax seeds with water and set aside.

2. In another bowl, mix the flours, baking powder and baking soda, as well as cinnamon and ground ginger. In another bowl, mix the yogurt, orange juice, agave syrup and sugar.

3. Pour this mixture over the dry ingredients then add the flax seeds and a pinch of salt.

4. Pour this batter into a round cake pan that has been lined with parchment paper.

5. Bake the cake at 350F for 40-50 minutes and serve sprinkled with powdered sugar.

Banana Coffee Cake

Banana coffee cake doesn't mean the cake contains coffee, but the cake is being layered with cinnamon sugar then baked until the layers blend together, creating a nice slice when cut.

Servings: 4-6 dishes

Ingredients:

1 tablespoons flax seeds, ground

2 tablespoons water

1/4 cup sugar

3/4 cup soy yogurt

1/3 cup soy milk

1 teaspoon vanilla extract

1/3 cup agave nectar

1 teaspoon cinnamon

1 cup all purpose flour

1/2 cup whole wheat flour

1 teaspoon baking powder

2 ripe bananas, mashed

1 pinch of salt

Directions:

1. Grease a 9 inch round pan and turn your oven on. Set the temperature to 350F.

2. In a small bowl, mix the ground seeds with water and set aside to soak. In another bowl, mix the sugar with cinnamon and set aside.

3. Mix the soy yogurt with milk, vanilla extract and agave nectar. Stir in the flax seeds then the flour, baking powder and a pinch of salt. Mix well then fold in the mashed bananas. Pour the batter into the pan and sprinkle the sugar mixed with cinnamon.

4. Bake in the preheated oven for 40-50 minutes. Let it cool in the pan then transfer to a serving plate.

Date and Walnut Cake

Dates and walnuts complement each other perfectly because they both have an earthy flavor so the final cake is absolutely delicious and moist.

Servings: 4-6 dishes

Ingredients:

1 2/3 cups whole wheat flour
1/4 cup all purpose flour
1/2 cup coconut oil
3/4 cup sugar
1 cup soy milk
1 cup water
1 cup dates, pitted
1/2 cup walnuts
1 teaspoon instant coffee
2 tablespoons cocoa powder
1/4 cup cocoa nibs
1 teaspoon baking powder
1/2 teaspoon baking soda
1 pinch of salt

Directions:

1. Grease or line with parchment paper a 9 inch round pan. Pour the milk into a small saucepan and bring to the boiling point. Remove from heat and stir in the instant coffee and cocoa powder. Add the pitted dates and let it stand for 20 minutes.

2. In a bowl, mix the flours with the baking powder, baking soda and a pinch of salt. Add the sugar then pour in the milk and dates, the water and oil. Mix well then fold in the walnuts.

3. Pour the batter into the prepared pan and bake in a preheated oven at 350F for 50 minutes. Serve sprinkled with powdered sugar.

Chocolate Zucchini Cake

Zucchini in a cake! You may think it's weird; but think about carrot cake, it's pretty much the same. Zucchinis don't have an overpowering flavor so the cake tastes more like chocolate, but still has more moisture and creaminess than other cakes.

Servings: 4-6 dishes

Ingredients:
1 cup whole wheat flour
1 cup all purpose flour
1 teaspoon baking powder 1/2 cup coconut oil 1/2 cup applesauce
1/2 cup sugar
1/2 cup brown sugar
2 tablespoons flax seeds, ground
4 tablespoons water
1 medium size zucchini, grated
1/2 cup cocoa powder
1 teaspoon instant coffee
1/4 cup coconut milk
1 pinch of salt

Directions:

1. In a small cup or bowl, mix the ground flax seeds with water and let them soak.

2. In a bowl, mix together the flours, cocoa, baking soda and powder as well as a pinch of salt.

3. In another bowl, mix the coconut oil with the applesauce, sugars and instant coffee.

4. Stir in the flax seeds then the flour mixture. Fold in the zucchini and pour the batter into a 9-inch greased cake pan.

5. Bake in a preheated oven at 350F for 40-50 minutes.

6. Let it cool in the pan then transfer to a serving plate and sprinkle with plenty of powdered sugar.

Cranberry Carrot Cake

Cranberries used in this cake are fresh so the cake is very flavorful and a bit tangy. The cranberries are like small delights hidden in the batter.

Servings: 4-6 dishes

Ingredients:

3 cups all purpose flour

1 cup sugar

1 teaspoon baking powder

1/2 teaspoon baking soda

1 pinch of salt

10 oz crushed pineapple

1 cup unsweetened applesauce

3/4 cup soy yogurt

1/4 cup coconut oil

1 cup shredded carrots

1 cup fresh cranberries

Directions:

1. In a bowl, sift together the flour, baking powder, soda and salt. Add the sugar.

2. In another bowl, mix the crushed pineapple, applesauce, yogurt and oil then pour this mixture over the dry ingredients. Mix well.

3. Fold in the shredded or grated carrots and the fresh cranberries.

4. Pour this batter into a round cake pan or a loaf pan and bake in a preheated oven at 350F for 30-40 minutes or until a skewer inserted in the center of the cake comes out clean.

5. Serve when cold with a generous sprinkle of powdered sugar.

Orange Poppy Seed Cake

Poppy seed cakes are a classic. This particular recipe uses orange as the second flavor so the final result has a strong aroma and an incredible taste.

Servings: 4-6 dishes

Ingredients:

2 oranges

2 bananas

3 tablespoons poppy seeds

2 1/2 cups almond meal

1/4 cup all purpose flour

3/4 teaspoon baking powder

2 tablespoons coconut oil

1 pinch of salt

Directions:

1. Pour a few cups of water in a medium size pan and throw in the oranges, whole.

2. Bring to a boil and simmer on low heat for 1-2 hours until soft. Drain and let them cool. Cut them into large chunks and remove the seeds, if any, then put them in a blender with the. Pulse a few times until well blended.

3. In another bowl, mix together the almond meal with flour and baking powder, as well as a pinch of salt. Pour in the orange mixture and give it a good stir. Fold in the poppy seeds and pour the batter into a greased 9-inch round pan.

4. Bake in a preheated oven at 375F for 40-50 minutes.

Lemon Poppy Seed Cake

Lemon combined with poppy seeds is an all-time duo that most people like due to its interesting, tangy flavor and crunchy texture.

Servings: 4-6 dishes

Ingredients:

2 cups all purpose flour

3 tablespoons poppy seeds

1 1/2 teaspoons baking powder

1/2 teaspoon baking soda

1 pinch of salt

2/3 cup almond milk

1/2 cup brown sugar

3 tablespoons lemon juice

1 tablespoon lemon zest

1 teaspoon vanilla extract

1 pinch of salt

Directions:

1. In a bowl, mix the flour, baking powder, baking soda, salt and the poppy seeds.

2. In another bowl, mix together the wet ingredients: Almond milk, sugar, lemon juice, zest and vanilla extract. Combine the two mixtures and stir well.

3. Pour the batter into a greased small cake pan and bake in a preheated oven at 350F for 4050 minutes or until slightly golden brown.

Chocolate Banana Carrot Cake

Chocolate, bananas and carrots may seem like a lot to put in one cake, but they complement each other and the final result is surprisingly good.

Servings: 4-6 dishes

Ingredients:
4 bananas, mashed
2 large carrots, grated
1 3/4 cups flour
3/4 cup brown sugar
1 teaspoon baking powder
1 teaspoon baking soda
3/4 cup cocoa powder
1/2 cup coconut oil
1 cup coconut milk
1 teaspoon vanilla extract
1 pinch of salt

Directions:

1. In a bowl, mix the mashed bananas with the grated carrot then stir in the milk and coconut oil and also the vanilla extract.

2. In another bowl, sift the flour with the cocoa powder, baking powder and baking soda, as well as a pinch of salt.

3. Combine the dry ingredients with the wet ones and mix well.

4. Pour the batter into a round cake pan and bake in a preheated oven at 350F for 40-50 minutes.

5. Let it cool in the pan then transfer to a serving plate and sprinkle over a generous amount of powdered sugar before serving.

Coconut Cake with Caramel Sauce

Coconut and caramel taste great together and this cake is amazing due to that. If you like either coconut or caramel, you should really try this cake as you will not regret it.

Servings: 4-6 dishes

Ingredients:
1 1/2 cups whole wheat flour
1/4 cup all purpose flour
1 teaspoon baking powder
3/4 teaspoon baking soda
1/2 cup sugar
1 cup coconut milk
1/3 coconut oil
1 teaspoon lemon juice
1 tablespoon flax seeds, ground
2 tablespoons waterFor the caramel sauce:
1 cup sugar
2 tablespoons coconut oil
1/2 cup water

Directions:

1. In a bowl, mix together the two types of flour with the baking powder and soda, but also the sugar and a pinch of salt. In another bowl, mix the lemon juice with the flax seeds and water.

2. Let them soak for 5 minutes then stir in the coconut milk and coconut oil. Add the dry ingredients and give it a good mix to combine well.

3. Grease a round cake pan then pour the batter into the pan.

4. Bake in a preheated oven at 375F for 30-40 minutes.

5. To make the sauce: Melt the sugar in a heavy saucepan. When it has an amber color, stir in the coconut oil then pour in the water. Mix well until smooth then remove from heat.

6. Serve the cake with a drizzle of caramel sauce.

Cardamom Carrot Cake

Carrot cake is a classic, but you can add a little twist if you are adventurous. This recipe uses a bit of cardamom to spice it up and create an amazing cake for you to enjoy.

Servings: 4-6 dishes

Ingredients:
1 1/2 cups whole wheat flour
1 cup all purpose flour
1 teaspoon baking powder
1 teaspoon baking soda
1 teaspoon ground cardamom
1/2 teaspoon cinnamon
1 teaspoon lemon juice
1/2 cup soy yogurt 1/2 cup applesauce 1 cup maple syrup
1/2 cup coconut oil
2 cups grated carrots
1 teaspoon vanilla extract
1 pinch of salt

Directions:

1. In a large bowl, sift the flours with baking soda, baking powder, cardamom and lemon juice, as well as a pinch of salt. In another bowl, mix the lemon juice, yogurt, applesauce, maple syrup, vanilla and coconut oil.

2. Combine the two mixtures then fold in the grated carrots.

3. Pour the batter into a greased 9-inch cake pan then bake in a preheated oven at 350F for 40-50 minutes or until a skewer inserted in the middle of the cake comes out clean.

4. Serve sprinkled with powdered sugar.

Mandarin Cake

Mandarins are similar to oranges, but their flavor is a bit different. This cake is easy to make and perfect as a dessert, topped with coconut cream or as an afternoon snack.

Servings: 2-4 dishes

Ingredients:
1 cup all purpose flour
3/4 cup whole wheat flour
1/2 cup brown sugar
1 teaspoon baking soda
1 cup mandarin juice
1/4 cup coconut milk
1/4 cup coconut oil
1 pinch of salt
1 teaspoon vanilla extract

Directions:

1. In a bowl, mix the flours with baking soda, salt and brown sugar.

2. Stir in the mandarin juice, then the coconut milk, oil and vanilla extract.

3. Grease a 9-inch cake pan and pour the batter into the pan.

4. Bake in a preheated oven at 350F for 40-50 minutes, or until slightly golden brown and fragrant.

Chocolate Orange Cake

Chocolate and orange is one of the best combinations I can think of because the orange mellows down the flavor of the chocolate, while the chocolate enhances the flavor of the orange.

Servings: 4-6 dishes

Ingredients:
1 1/2 cups all purpose flour
1 cup whole wheat flour
1/2 cup cornstarch
1 1/2 cups sugar
1 teaspoon baking soda
1/2 cup cocoa powder
3/4 cup soy yogurt
1 teaspoon cinnamon
1/2 cup fresh orange juice
1 tablespoon orange zest
1 teaspoon vanilla extract
1 pinch of salt

Directions:

1. In a large bowl, combine the flour with the sugar, cornstarch, baking soda and cocoa powder.

2. Stir in the soy yogurt, cinnamon, orange juice, vanilla extract, salt and orange zest. Beat well with a hand mixer for 2 minutes then pour the batter into a greased round cake pan.

3. Bake in a preheated oven at 350F for 30-40 minutes.

4. To serve, glaze with chocolate, melted with a few tablespoons of butter or heavy cream.

Peach Upside-Down Cake

Upside down cakes are great because the fruits on the bottom turn very soft and they are similar to a cream so, when you turn the cake upside down, the top will be very silky and juicy, infusing the batter underneath as well.

Servings: 4-6 dishes

Ingredients:
1 1/2 cups all purpose flour
1 teaspoon baking powder
1 teaspoon cinnamon
1 teaspoon ground ginger
1/2 cup sugar
1 pinch of salt
1 cup soy milk
1 teaspoon lemon juice
1 teaspoon lemon zest
1 pound peaches, cut into slices
2 tablespoons brown sugar

Directions:

1. In a bowl, combine the flour with baking powder, cinnamon, ginger, sugar and salt. In another bowl, pour in the soy milk and lemon juice.

2. Mix well and let it stand for 5 minutes. Pour this over the flour then fold in the lemon zest.

3. Grease a heavy skillet with oil and sprinkle the brown sugar on the bottom. Arrange the peach slices over the sugar then spoon over the batter.

4. Bake in a preheated oven at 350F for 30-40 minutes. When done, remove from oven, let it cool in the pan for 10 minutes then turn the cake on a serving plate.

Pineapple Upside-Down Cake

Pineapple is amongst the most used fruits when it comes to upside down cakes because it's juicy, but not overly juicy and it bakes to perfection each time.

Servings: 4-6 dishes

Ingredients:
1 can pineapple slices, drained
1 cup quick oats
1 cup whole wheat flour
1/2 cup sugar
1 teaspoon baking powder
1 tablespoons flax seeds ground
2 tablespoons water
1 teaspoon cinnamon
1 teaspoon ground ginger
1 pinch of salt
1 teaspoon vanilla extract
1/3 cup unsweetened applesauce
3 tablespoons water
1 teaspoon lemon juice

Directions:

1. In a bowl, mix together the flax seeds with water and let them soak for 5 minutes. Add the applesauce, water, vanilla and lemon juice.

2. Stir in the quick oats, flour, sugar, baking powder, cinnamon and ginger, as well as a pinch of salt. Grease a 9-inch round cake pan and arrange the pineapple slices on the bottom.

3. Spoon the batter over the pineapple and bake in a preheated oven at 350F for 30-40 minutes. When done, remove from oven and let it cool for 10 minutes. Turn the cake on a serving plate and serve when chilled.

Raspberry Chocolate Cake

Chocolate works with any fruits, but with raspberries this cake turns into a real delight, able to awaken your senses with its strong flavors.

Servings: 4-6 dishes

Ingredients:

3 cups all purpose flour

1 cup sugar

2 teaspoons baking soda

1/2 cup cocoa

1/4 cup coconut oil

1/2 cup raspberry jam

1/4 cup applesauce, unsweetened

2 teaspoons white wine vinegar

2 cups water

1 pinch of salt

1/2 cup raspberry jam to glaze

Directions:

1. In a bowl, mix the flour with the sugar, baking soda, cocoa and a pinch of salt.

2. Stir in the oil, raspberry jam, applesauce, water and white wine vinegar. Using a hand mixer, beat for 2 minutes then pour the batter into a 9-inch round cake pan, lined with parchment paper.

3. Bake the cake in a preheated oven for 30-40 minutes or until a skewer inserted in the cake comes out clean.

4. Remove from oven and let it cool in the pan. Once cold, cut it in half lengthwise then spread raspberry jam between the cake layers.

Cherry, Walnut and Banana Cake

Basically, this is a banana and walnut cake, but the addition of cherries improves its texture and gives it a bit more freshness. It's also a combination of earthy flavors and spring, fresh aromas.

Servings: 4-6 dishes

Ingredients:
3 ripe bananas, mashed
2 teaspoons lemon juice
1/4 cup unsweetened applesauce
1/2 cup brown sugar
1 cup whole wheat flour
1 cup all purpose flour
1/2 cup dried cherries
1 teaspoon baking powder
1 teaspoon baking soda
2/3 cup walnuts, chopped
1 pinch of salt

Directions:

1. Mix the bananas with the lemon juice in a bowl.

2. Stir in the applesauce and sugar then add the flours, baking powder, baking soda and salt. Mix well to combine and fold in the dried cherries and walnuts.

3. Pour the batter into a greased round cake pan and bake in a preheated oven at 350F for 4050 minutes or until slightly golden brown and fragrant.

4. Serve cold with a generous sprinkling of powdered sugar.

Cherry Snack Cake

Incorporating rolled oats, this cake makes an excellent choice for breakfast, but it also works as a snack and it's delicious.

Servings: 4-6 dishes

Ingredients:

1 cup rolled oats

1 tablespoon flax seeds

1 1/2 cup whole wheat flour

1 teaspoon baking powder

1 teaspoon baking soda

1/2 teaspoon all spice powder

1/3 cup maple syrup

1/2 cup cherry juice

1 cup pitted cherries

1/2 cup applesauce

1 pinch of salt

Directions:

1. Put the oats and flax seeds in a food processor or blender and pulse a few times until ground.

2. Transfer to a bowl and stir in the flour, baking powder and baking soda, as well as the all spice powder and a pinch of salt. Add the cherry juice, maple syrup and applesauce. Fold in the pitted cherries and pour the batter into a greased small cake pan.

3. Bake in a preheated oven at 350F for 40-50 minutes or until a skewer inserted in the center of the cake comes out clean.

Chocolate Zucchini Mud Cake

Moist and creamy, this cake proves that healthy baking can be done with vegetables as well. Don't be put off by the use of zucchinis because they make this cake as delicious as it is.

Servings: 4-6 dishes

Ingredients:
2 cups whole wheat flour
1 1/2 cup raw sugar
3/4 cup cocoa powder
3/4 cup chickpea flour
1 teaspoon baking soda
1/2 teaspoon baking powder
1 pinch of salt
3/4 cup coconut oil
1 cup water
1 1/2 cups grated zucchini
1 teaspoon vanilla extract
1 teaspoon cinnamon

Directions:

1. In a bowl, mix the flour with the raw sugar, cocoa powder, chickpea flour, baking soda, baking powder, salt and cinnamon.

2. Stir in the coconut oil, water, vanilla and grated zucchini. Mix well then spoon the batter into a greased bund pan and bake in a preheated oven at 350F for 1 hour or until a toothpick inserted in the middle of the cake comes out clean.

3. When done, let the cake cool in the pan then transfer to a wire rack. If you want, you can glaze it with melted vegan chocolate.

Vegan Basic Vanilla Cake

This is probably one of the most basic recipes and it can be a good base for other desserts as you can fill it with jam or cream, frost it and transform it into a beautiful celebration cake.

Servings: 4-6 dishes

Ingredients:

3/4 cup brown rice flour

1/2 cup tapioca flour

1/2 cup almond meal

1/2 cup coconut flour

1 pinch of salt

1 teaspoon baking powder

1 teaspoon baking soda

1 teaspoon xanthan gum

2/3 cup coconut milk

1 cup water 1/4 cup coconut oil 1/4 cup applesauce

1 tablespoon vanilla extract

1 teaspoon lemon juice

Directions:

1. In a bowl, mix all the flours with the salt, baking powder, baking soda and xanthan gum.

2. In another bowl, combine the water with the coconut milk, coconut oil, applesauce, vanilla extract and lemon juice. Pour it over the flour and mix until smooth.

3. Grease a 9-inch cake pan or line it with baking paper then pour the batter into the pan.

4. Bake in a preheated oven at 350F for 1 hour or until a skewer inserted in the middle of the cake comes out clean. Let it cool in the pan before serving.

Olive Oil Rosemary Semolina Cake

Although it sounds more like a savory cake, it's not. In fact, it's such a flavorful and delicious day to day dessert that you will save the recipe for a next time as well.

Serving: 4-6 dishes

Ingredients:

2/3 cup olive oil

2 tablespoons chopped rosemary

1 pinch of salt

3 cups warm water

3 1/2 cups semolina flour

3 tablespoons ground flax seeds

Juice from 1 orange

1 cup sugar

Directions:

1. Pour the olive oil into a saucepan and heat it. Add the rosemary then let it infuse 20 minutes. Drain and discard the rosemary.

2. In a bowl, mix the yeast with the warm water and let it bloom for 10 minutes.

3. Stir in the orange juice, sugar, flax seeds and semolina flour, as well as a pinch of salt.

4. Let it soak for 10 minutes then add the olive oil. Cover the bowl and let the batter rise forat least 2 hours.

5. Grease a bundt pan with oil and flour it slightly then pour the risen batter into the pan.

6. Bake in a preheated oven at 350F for 40-60 minutes or until risen and golden brown. Let it cool in the pan before serving.

Apfelkuchen

Apfelkuchen is a German recipe and it translates to apple cake. The recipe is vegan and it yields an outstanding, flavorful and delicious cake.

Servings: 4-6 dishes

Ingredients:
2 pounds apples, peeled, cored and sliced
1/2 cup solid coconut oil
1/2 cup raw sugar
1/2 cup applesauce
1/4 cup soy milk
2 teaspoons baking powder
1 cup whole wheat flour
1/2 cup all purpose flour
1 pinch of salt
1 teaspoon cinnamon

Directions:

1. In a bowl, mix the coconut oil with the sugar until creamy then stir in the applesauce and soy milk. Add the flours, salt and baking powder, then spoon the batter into a 9-inch baking pan, greased or lined with baking paper.

2. Top the batter with apple slices and sprinkle with cinnamon.

3. Bake in a preheated oven at 375F for 30-40 minutes. Let it cool in the pan before serving.

Blueberry Chocolate Cake

Blueberries and chocolate come together in this recipe to create one of the best cakes you will ever taste. It's moist and fragrant, absolutely delicious and it's worth a try.

Servings: 4-6 dishes

Ingredients:
1 cups whole wheat flour
1/4 cup all purpose flour
1/4 cup cocoa powder
1 teaspoon baking powder
1/2 teaspoon baking soda
1 teaspoon ground flax seeds
3/4 cup water
1/2 cup maple syrup
1 cup blueberries
1 pinch of salt

Directions:

1. In a medium bowl, mix the flours, cocoa powder, baking powder, soda and salt, as well as the ground flax seeds.

2. Pour the water into a blender and add the blueberries. Pulse a few times until smooth. Stir this mixture into the dry ingredients, together with the maple syrup.

3. Pour the batter into a greased medium-size cake pan. Bake in a preheated oven at 350F for 40-50 minutes.

4. Serve sprinkled with powdered sugar and a pinch of cinnamon.

Blueberry Whole Wheat Muffins

These muffins are not only delicious, but also very healthy due to their high content of fiber and antioxidants. The blueberries can easily be replaced with strawberries or raspberries if you wish to customize the recipe to your own taste and preference.

Servings: 12 muffins

Ingredients:

1½ cups whole wheat flour

½ cup oat flour

2 teaspoons baking soda

1 pinch salt

½ cup agave syrup

2 tablespoons ground flax seeds

¼ cup water

½ cup coconut oil, melted

½ cup almond milk

1 teaspoon apple cider vinegar

1 cup fresh or frozen blueberries

Directions:

1. In a bowl, mix the flour with the oat flour, baking soda and salt. Set aside.
2. In a different bowl, combine the flax seeds with the water.
3. Allow them to soak for 10 minutes then add the agave syrup, coconut oil, almond milk, and cider vinegar.
4. Stir in the dry ingredients you mixed earlier and give it a good stir.
5. Gently fold in the blueberries and spoon the batter into your muffin cups lined with muffin papers.
6. Bake in a preheated oven at 350°F for 20-30 minutes or until slightly goldenbrown and fragrant. Allow the muffins to cool in the pan before serving.

Chocolate Chip Cookie Dough Muffins

The dough for these muffins is similar to a cookie, so the final muffins are a bit denser but just as delicious. Actually the taste of these cookies certainly makes you think about chocolate chip cookies!

Servings: 6 muffins

Ingredients

½ cup pecans, ground

½ cup shredded coconut

¼ cup almond butter

2 tablespoons flax seeds, ground

¼ cup coconut milk

¼ cup agave syrup

1 vanilla extract

¼ cup vegan chocolate chips

Directions:

1. Mix the almond butter with the agave syrup until creamy.
2. Stir in the coconut milk, and then add the pecans, coconut, flax seeds, and vanilla.
3. Fold in the chocolate chips then spoon the batter into muffin cups lined with muffin papers.
4. Bake in a preheated oven at 350°F for 25 minutes or until golden brown and fragrant.
5. Serve these muffins once they have cooled fully.

Banana and Sunflower Muffins

Servings: 12 muffins

Ingredients: *2 tablespoons ground flax seeds*

¼ cup cold water

1 cup oat flour

¼ cup cornstarch

½ cup almond flour

½ cup sunflower seeds, ground

1 pinch salt

1 teaspoon baking powder

½ cup sunflower oil

2 ripe bananas, mashed

½ cup maple syrup

Directions:

1. In a bowl, mix the ground flax seeds with the cold water and allow them to soak for 10 minutes.
2. Stir in the mashed bananas, sunflower oil, and maple syrup.
3. In a different bowl, combine the oat flour, cornstarch, almond flour, ground sunflower seeds, salt, and baking powder.
4. Stir in the wet ingredients and mix well. Spoon the batter into your muffin cups and bake in a preheated oven at 350°F for 20 minutes or until golden brown and fragrant.

Fudgy Chocolate Muffins

The special ingredient of these muffins is the beet purée which adds an interesting earthy flavor and makes them fudgy and delicious. You can customize this recipe any way you want in terms of flavors: add dark rum or some fresh fruit if you wish.

Servings: 12 muffins

Ingredients:

2 tablespoons ground flax seeds

2 tablespoons water

1 large beet, pureed in a blender

¼ cup agave syrup

¼ cup maple syrup

¼ cup coconut oil

¼ cup coconut milk

1 pinch salt

1 teaspoon baking soda

½ cup cocoa powder

1 cup all-purpose flour

½ cup oat flour

Directions:

1. Mix the flax seeds with the water, beet purée, agave syrup, maple syrup, coconut oil, and coconut milk in a bowl.
2. Stir in the rest of the ingredients and mix really well.
3. Spoon the batter into your muffin cups and bake in a preheated oven at 350°Ffor 20 minutes or until golden brown and fragrant.
4. When done, remove the muffins from the oven and allow them to cool in the pan before serving.

Tropical Coconut Muffins

This recipe focuses on the amazing mix and taste of coconut, pineapple, and mango to create a moist and delicious dessert using healthy ingredients. Feel free to use different fruits though; it's entirely up to you!

Servings: 12 muffins

Ingredients:

1½ cups rolled oats

1½ cups oat flour

½ cup coconut flakes

1 teaspoon baking powder

1 teaspoon baking soda

1 pinch salt

½ cup soy yogurt

½ cup coconut cream

½ cup maple syrup

¼ cup coconut oil

1 ripe banana, mashed

½ cup crushed pineapple, drained

½ cup mango dices

Directions:

1. Mix the rolled oats with the oat flour, coconut flakes, baking powder, baking soda, and salt. Set aside.

2. In a different bowl, mix the soy yogurt, coconut cream, maple syrup, coconut oil, and banana. Pour this mixture over the dry ingredients and give it a good mix.

3. Fold in the pineapple and mango then spoon the batter into your muffin cupslined with muffin papers.

4. Bake in a preheated oven at 350°F for 20-25 minutes or until golden brown and fluffy. Remove the muffins from the oven and serve them once they have cooled down.

Melon Muffins

Melons or cantaloupes are the staple of summer with their lovely, intense flavor, but you can use that flavor to create delicious desserts too, such as these moist muffins.

Servings: 12 muffins

Ingredients:
1 cup whole wheat flour
½ cup all-purpose flour
1 teaspoon baking soda
1 pinch salt
1 pinch ground ginger
1 small melon, peeled and cubed
¼ cup agave syrup
1 teaspoon vanilla extract
¼ cup coconut oil

Directions:

1. Mix the melon with the agave syrup, vanilla and coconut oil in a blender.
2. Purée until smooth and then stir in the flours, baking soda, salt, and ginger.
3. Spoon the batter into your muffin cups lined with muffin papers and bake in a preheated oven at 350°F for 25 minutes or until the surface turns golden brown.

Multigrain Muffins

Multigrain automatically means that these muffins contain a multitude of nutrients and fiber, and are therefore perfect for breakfast. Served with a cup of tea or a glass of fresh juice in the morning, you can start your day on a high note.

Servings: 12 muffins

Ingredients:
2 tablespoons ground flax seeds
2 tablespoons cold water
1 cup almond milk
1 teaspoon apple cider vinegar
1½ cups all-purpose flour
¾ cup rolled oats
½ cup quinoa
1 teaspoon baking powder
1 pinch salt
½ teaspoon cinnamon powder
1½ cups pumpkin purée
½ cup maple syrup
¼ cup pumpkin seeds
¼ cup sunflower seeds
2 tablespoons poppy seeds

Directions:

1. In a bowl, mix the flax seeds with the cold water.
2. After 5 minutes of soaking, stir in the almond milk, vinegar, pumpkin purée, and maple syrup.
3. Stir in the flour, rolled oats, quinoa, baking powder, salt, and cinnamon powder.
4. Fold in the pumpkin seeds, sunflower seeds, and poppy seeds.
5. Spoon the batter into your muffin cups lined with muffin papers and bake in a preheated oven at 350°F for 25-30 minutes or until golden brown and fragrant.
6. Allow the muffins to cool in the pan before serving or storing.

Almond Cranberry Muffins

How about a fluffy, fragrant muffin for breakfast or your afternoon snack?! These muffins sure are perfect with their moist inside and crunchy, flavorful topping.

Servings: 12 muffins

Ingredients:

2 cups rolled oats
1 ripe banana, mashed
1 cup pumpkin purée
¼ cup almond butter
¼ cup almond milk
¼ cup maple syrup
½ cup dried cranberries, chopped
¼ teaspoon cinnamon powder
1 pinch salt
½ teaspoon baking soda
½ cup sliced almonds for topping

Directions:

1. Mix the mashed banana with the pumpkin purée, almond butter, almond milk, and maple syrup.
2. Stir in the rolled oats, cranberries, cinnamon, and salt as well as the bakingsoda.
3. Spoon the mixture into your muffin cups and top with sliced almonds.
4. Bake in a preheated oven at 350°F for 25-30 minutes or until crunchy and golden brown.
5. Allow the muffins to cool in the pan before serving.

Ginger and Banana Muffins

It's not unusual to combine ginger with bananas, but these muffins certainly bring out the most from this combination. They are moist like any banana muffin, but they are also special with their mild, lovely ginger aroma.

Servings: 12 muffins

Ingredients:

2¼ cups all-purpose flour

1 teaspoon baking soda

1 teaspoon baking powder

1 pinch salt

1 teaspoon ground ginger ⅓ cup coconut oil ½ cup applesauce

2 ripe bananas, mashed

⅔ cup coconut milk

Directions:

1. Combine the flour with the baking soda, baking powder, and salt. Stir in the ginger, coconut oil applesauce, bananas, and coconut milk.
2. Spoon the batter into your muffin cups and bake in a preheated oven at 350°F for 20-30 minutes or until fragrant and golden brown.
3. Allow the muffins to cool completely before serving or storing.

Plum Muffins

Plums are so underestimated. These muffins not only emphasize the taste of the plums, but also their juiciness and deliciousness. However, you can use other fruits if you prefer.

Servings: 12 muffins

Ingredients:

1¾ cups oat flour

1 pinch salt

1 teaspoon baking soda

½ teaspoon cinnamon powder

½ cup agave syrup

1 cup silken tofu

1 teaspoon vanilla extract

¼ cup coconut oil, melted

2 tablespoons ground flax seeds

8 plums, pitted and diced

Directions:

1. Mix the oat flour with the salt, baking soda and cinnamon and set aside.
2. In a blender, combine the silken tofu with the agave syrup, vanilla extract, coconut oil, and flax seeds.
3. Pour this mixture over the dry ingredients and mix well.
4. Fold in the plums then spoon the batter into your muffin cups lined with muffin papers and bake in a preheated oven at 350°F for 25 minutes or until risen and golden brown.

Blackberry Corn Muffins

The cornstarch makes these muffins slightly grainier, but they are still delicious and moist due to the cranberries which infuse the corn batter with their taste.

Servings: 12 muffins

Ingredients:

1 cup cornstarch
1 cup all-purpose flour
1 teaspoon baking powder
1 pinch cinnamon powder
1 pinch salt
¾ cup applesauce
1 cup coconut milk
½ cup agave syrup
1 teaspoon vanilla extract
1 cup blackberries

Directions:

1. Combine the flours with the baking powder, cinnamon, and salt. Stir in the applesauce, coconut milk, agave syrup, and vanilla.
2. Fold in the blackberries then spoon the batter into your muffin pan lined with muffin papers.
3. Bake in a preheated oven at 350°F for 20-30 minutes.
4. To check that these muffins are cooked through, insert a toothpick in the center of one muffin.
5. If it comes out clean, the muffins are ready, if it comes out with traces of batter, then the muffins require a few more minutes baking. 6. Allow the muffins to cool in the pan when ready.

Sweet Potato Ginger Muffins

I'm sure you've had pumpkin muffins before, but sweet potato has a similar consistency so why not use it in baking as well? The final muffins are fragrant and moist, but also rich and filling.

Servings: 12 muffins

Ingredients:

2 cups whole wheat flour

1 teaspoon baking soda

1 pinch salt

1 teaspoon cinnamon powder ½ teaspoon ground cloves 1 teaspoon grated ginger

1 teaspoon vanilla extract

½ cup coconut oil

2 tablespoons ground flax seeds

½ cup almond milk

½ cup maple syrup

1 large sweet potato, baked and mashed

1 sweet potato, peeled and grated

½ cup pecans, chopped

Directions:

1. In a bowl, mix the flour with the baking soda, salt, cinnamon, ground cloves, and flax seeds. Set aside.
2. In a different bowl, combine the coconut oil, grated ginger, vanilla, milk, maple syrup, and baked sweet potato.
3. Stir in the dry ingredients then fold in the grated sweet potato and the choppedpecans.
4. Spoon the batter into your muffin cups lined with muffin papers.
5. Bake in a preheated oven at 350°F for 20-25 minutes or until golden brown and fragrant. Allow the muffins to cool in the pan before serving.

Quinoa Raspberry Muffins

Quinoa is the super food of the century, but apart from using it as and in savory dishes, it can also be added to your desserts to boost the nutritional content.

Servings: 12 muffins

Ingredients:

½ cup quinoa, toasted

½ cup orange juice

2 cups all-purpose flour

½ cup cornstarch

1½ teaspoons baking powder

1 pinch salt

½ cup agave syrup

2 tablespoons orange zest

1 cup almond milk

½ cup orange juice

¼ cup coconut oil, melted

1 teaspoon vanilla extract

1½ cups fresh raspberries

Directions:

1. In a bowl, mix the quinoa with the half cup of orange juice and allow to soak overnight if you can, although this isn't compulsory.
2. Stir in the agave syrup, almond milk, orange zest, the other half cup of orange juice, coconut oil, and vanilla.
3. Incorporate the flour, cornstarch, salt, and baking powder.
4. Give it a good mix then fold in the raspberries.
5. Spoon the batter into your muffin cups lined with muffin papers and bake in a preheated oven at 350°F for 20-30 minutes or until golden brown and well risen.
6. Allow the muffins to cool in the pan before serving.

Applesauce Cardamom Muffins

The applesauce in these muffins pairs wonderfully with the ground cardamom. You can also add a few dices of fresh apple if you wish to enhance the taste and flavors.

Servings: 12 muffins

Ingredients:
1 cup coconut milk
1 cup applesauce
¼ cup agave syrup
1 teaspoon lemon juice
2 tablespoons ground flax seeds
1 pinch salt
1 teaspoon baking soda
1 teaspoon ground ginger
1 teaspoon ground cardamom
1½ cups all-purpose flour
½ cup almond flour

Directions:

1. In a bowl, mix the coconut milk with the applesauce, agave syrup, and lemon juice.
2. Stir in the flax seeds, flours, salt, baking soda, ground ginger, and cardamom.
3. Spoon the batter into your muffin pan and bake them in a preheated oven at 350°F for 30 minutes or until golden brown and fragrant. Serve these muffins once cooled.

www.ingramcontent.com/pod-product-compliance
Lightning Source LLC
Chambersburg PA
CBHW070915080526
44589CB00013B/1296